A Note to Parents

DK READERS is a compelling program for beginning readers, designed in conjunction with leading literacy experts, including Dr. Linda Gambrell, Distinguished Professor of Education at Clemson University. Dr. Gambrell has served as President of the National Reading Conference, the College Reading Association, and the International Reading Association.

Beautiful illustrations and superb full-color photographs combine with engaging, easy-to-read stories to offer a fresh approach to each subject in the series. Each DK READER is guaranteed to capture a child's interest while developing his or her reading skills, general knowledge, and love of reading.

The five levels of DK READERS are aimed at different reading abilities, enabling you to choose the books that are exactly right for your child:

Pre-level 1: Learning to read
Level 1: Beginning to read
Level 2: Beginning to read alone
Level 3: Reading alone
Level 4: Proficient readers

The "normal" age at which a child begins to read can be anywhere from three to eight years old. Adult participation through the lower levels is very helpful for providing encouragement, discussing storylines, and sounding out unfamiliar words.

No matter which level you select, you can be sure that you are helping your child learn to read, then read to learn!

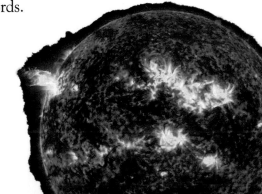

LONDON, NEW YORK, MUNICH,
MELBOURNE, and DELHI

DK LONDON
Series Editor Deborah Lock
US Senior Editor Shannon Beatty
Project Art Editor Ann Cannings
Producer, Pre-production Francesca Wardell

Reading Consultant
Linda Gambrell, Ph.D.

DK DELHI
Editor Pomona Zaheer
Assistant Art Editor Yamini Panwar
DTP Designers Anita Yadav, Vijay Kandwal
Picture Researcher Surya Sarangi
Deputy Managing Editor Soma B. Chowdhury

First American Edition, 2014
Published in the United States by DK Publishing
345 Hudson Street, New York, New York 10014

14 15 16 17 18 10 9 8 7 6 5 4 3 2 1
001—195868—August/14

A catalog record for this book is available
from the Library of Congress.

ISBN: 978-1-4654-2003-9 (Paperback)
ISBN: 978-1-4654-2002-2 (Hardback)

DK books are available at special discounts when purchased in bulk
for sales promotions, premiums, fund-raising, or educational use.
For details, contact:
DK Publishing Special Markets
345 Hudson Street, New York, New York 10014
SpecialSales@dk.com

Printed and bound in China
by South China Printing Company.

The publisher would like to thank the following for
their kind permission to reproduce their photographs:
(Key: a=above, b=below/bottom, c=center, l=left, r=right, t=top)
1 **NASA**: SDO (br). 2 **Dreamstime.com**: Julien Tromeur (br).
3 **Getty Images**: Stocktrek RF. 4–29 **NASA**: ESA and G. Bacon
(STScI) (b). 5 **NASA**: (t). 7 **Dreamstime.com**: Alexokokok (c/Frame);
Science Photo Library: Roger Harris (c). 8 **NASA**: JPL-Caltech (t);
Dreamstime.com: Julien Tromeur (clb). 9 **NASA**: (cb). 11 **NASA**:
JPL-Caltech (t). 12 **NASA**: JPL-Caltech (t). 15 **NASA**: JPL-Caltech (t).
16 **NASA**: JPL-Caltech/MSSS (t). 17 **Dreamstime.com**: Julien
Tromeur (crb). 18–19 **NASA**: JPL/Arizona State University (t).
20–21 **Corbis**: Michael Freeman (t). 23 **Corbis**: Tony Gervis/Robert
Harding World Imagery (t). 24 **NASA**: SDO (tc); **Dreamstime.com**:
Julien Tromeur (cla). 25 **Dreamstime.com**: Julien Tromeur (crb).
27 **Dreamstime.com**: Julien Tromeur (crb). 29 **NASA**: JPL (t).
30 **NASA**: CXC/JPL-Caltech/STScI (background); **NASA**:
JPL-Caltech (cr).
Jacket images: Front: Dreamstime.com: Jochen Schönfeld/Time123 (tc);
Fotolia: victorhabbick (b). **Back: NASA**: JPL-Caltech (tl), MOLA
Science Team/O. de Goursac, Adrian Lark (cr). **Spine: NASA**: MOLA
Science Team/O. de Goursac, Adrian Lark (b).

All other images © Dorling Kindersley
For further information see: www.dkimages.com.

Discover more at
www.dk.com

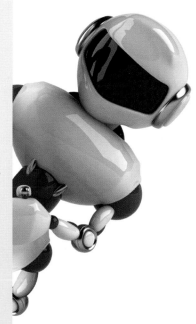

DK READERS

Space Quest
Mission to Mars

Written by Peter Lock

Year 2050

Five astronauts crawled into
the command capsule at the top
of a rocket. They were about
to set off on an exciting mission:
Space Quest.

The aim was to visit the planets of
the solar system to collect samples
and set up bases, if possible.
The first stage was to Mars.

Mission team

Name	Age	Role
Ned Crater	41	Commander
Flo Comet	32	Engineer
Alex Nova	35	Lander pilot
Izzy Stardust	29	Science officer
Lem Cosmos	28	Engineer
Coconut	3	Pet rabbit

"We have lift-off," said Ned.

The rocket zoomed upward. Jets of fire and billows of smoke blazed behind. The capsule shook violently.

In the hold, Coconut the pet rabbit lay curled up, resting in her special space hutch. She opened one eye, stirred, and then snuggled up again. This shaking was just like all the launch tests.

The rocket zoomed through the atmosphere. The launch engines dropped away.

As it entered outer space, the rocket leveled out. It sped toward the spacecraft *Ramesses*.

"Look guys! *Ramesses* is fantastic," said Flo, looking at the spacecraft ahead.

Ned took over the rocket's controls as they came close. He steered the rocket toward the docking hatch.

"Great steering, Ned," said Lem, as the rocket slid gently into the dock.

Ned pressed the switch to shut
down the rocket's engines.

"Welcome to your new home!"
said Ned.

After seven months traveling in space, *Ramesses* reached the outer atmosphere of Mars.

"We're now in orbit around Mars," announced Ned to CapCom. "We should be ready to go for the landing-capsule launch soon."

CapCom is for Capsule or Spacecraft Communicator. This is the only person at Mission Control on Earth who speaks with the astronauts.

Flo was helping Alex, Lem, and Izzy get into their suits for Mars.

"These boots will keep our feet cozy from the Martian cold," said Lem. He pulled on the boots with heated soles.

Once ready, they opened the hatch door and walked into the Mars lander, *Memphis*.

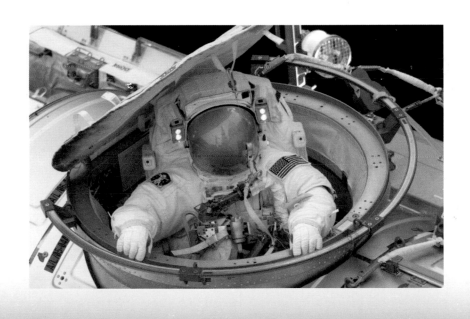

"Good luck," said Flo, waving goodbye to them as she closed the hatch. She and Ned were staying on board *Ramesses*.

Alex sat at the controls of *Memphis*. "Let's get this mission underway," he said. He guided *Memphis* away from the dock and rotated the heat shield toward the planet's surface.

"Are you ready for the ride of your lives?" he asked Lem and Izzy.

They nodded, but no one knew what the next six-minute attempt to land on Mars would be like.

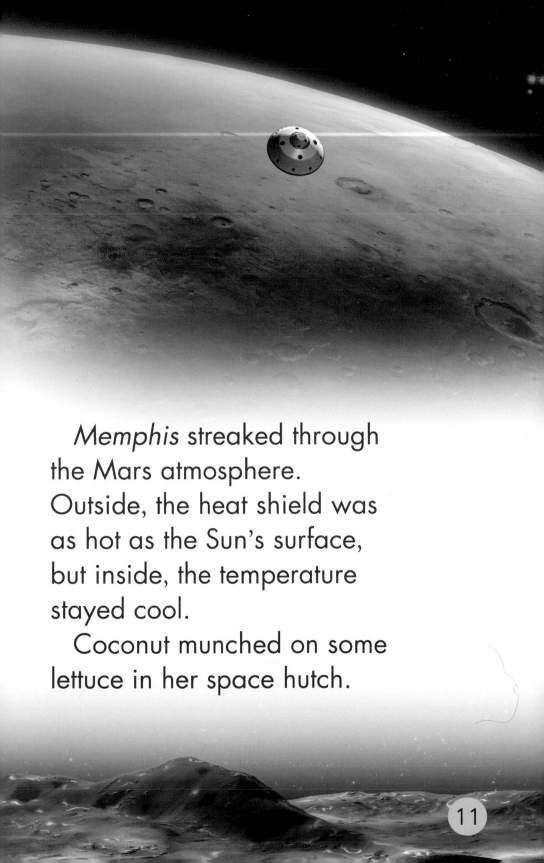

Memphis streaked through the Mars atmosphere. Outside, the heat shield was as hot as the Sun's surface, but inside, the temperature stayed cool.

Coconut munched on some lettuce in her space hutch.

Four minutes later, Alex
launched the huge parachute.
It billowed out behind *Memphis*,
slowing the lander down.

"This really is a strange colored sky," remarked Izzy. Mars was covered in an orange-red afternoon haze.

Suddenly, a strong gust of wind caught *Memphis*, and the lander swerved. They were right above a huge volcano. A fiery glowing lava flow oozed out of the crater below them.

"Alex, do something quickly," cried Izzy. "We're heading straight for that lava flow."

"I can't! The wind is too strong," said Alex. "We're out of control!"

Alex, Lem, and Izzy were being tossed around like clothes in a dryer.

Suddenly, the wind changed direction, lifting the lander's large parachute.

Memphis floated away from the danger of the main crater.

Alex regained control as the wind died down.

"Phew! Perhaps we can land more safely now."

At 50 feet (15 meters) above the surface, Alex fired the upward rockets. *Memphis* came to a complete stop.

The parachute detached, and wheels beneath the lander lowered. Alex fired short boosts of downward rockets. *Memphis* touched down on the surface.

"*Memphis* has landed," Alex said to CapCom.

Lem, Alex, and Izzy set up
the base first. They then started
exploring. They set off on their
quad bikes, which were specially
designed for moving over
the rocky Martian ground.

In a few hours, they reached
the edge of the great canyon, Valles
Marineris [VAL-less mar-uh-NAIR-iss].

Alex quickly set up
the monitoring equipment.

"I'm glad we have our suits on,"
said Alex. "The readings show
high levels of carbon dioxide.
We couldn't breathe on
our own in this thin air."

"We would choke on the fine
dust, too," added Lem.

The canyon **Valles Marineris** is
2,500 miles (4,000 km) long
and 4 miles (7 km) deep.
This canyon is the length of
the USA and seven times
deeper than the Grand Canyon.

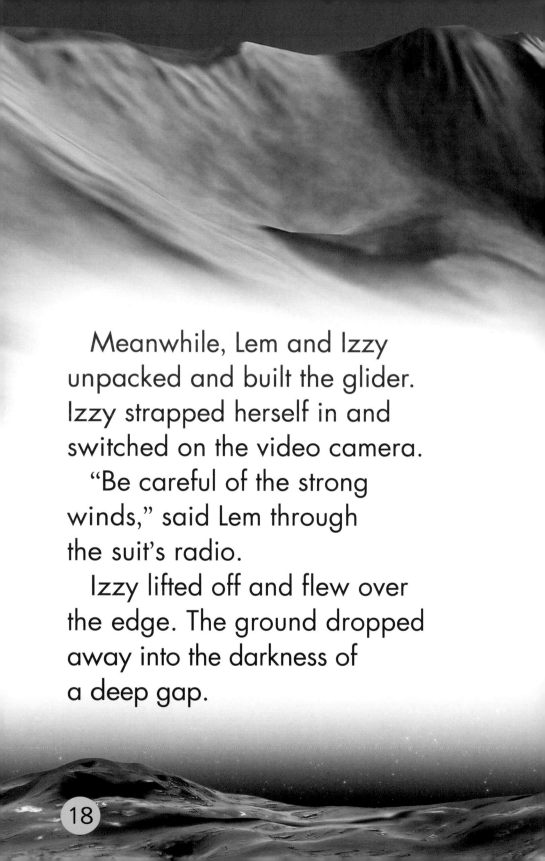

Meanwhile, Lem and Izzy unpacked and built the glider. Izzy strapped herself in and switched on the video camera.

"Be careful of the strong winds," said Lem through the suit's radio.

Izzy lifted off and flew over the edge. The ground dropped away into the darkness of a deep gap.

She soared along the canyon,
using the uplift of the swirling,
whirling wind currents.
She swooped over the towering
rocks, worn away by the wind.
She glided over giant landslides
and huge sand dunes.

"That was awesome, guys!" gasped Izzy, as she landed back with Lem and Alex.

Suddenly, Alex spotted a twirling and swirling twister of dust, speeding across the canyon.

"A colossal storm is coming straight for us," said Alex. "Let's get out of here—fast."

They jumped onto the quad bikes and sped away, but the twister was catching up with them.

"We're not going to make it back to base in time," cried Izzy. "We need to find some cover."

"What's that dark patch over there in the rocks?" asked Lem.

"That could be one of the Seven Sisters caves. Perfect!" called Alex.

They headed over to the cave as the twister sped closer.

As they reached the cave, they could feel the wind around their suits. They were nearly blown off the bikes. Izzy grabbed Coconut in her hutch. They all staggered to the cave opening. The darkness of the cave loomed.

Lem led the way as they entered the cave carefully.

"How far down does it go?" asked Alex, shouting over the screaming wind.

"I can't see the bottom. It could be a sheer drop," Lem shouted.

"There's a slight ledge with enough space for us to take shelter," suggested Izzy.

The storm whistled past
the cave entrance. Pieces of
dust and rocks were thrown
into the cave. They just missed
the cowering astronauts.
They waited until the twister had
passed before returning to the base.

Solar flares are sudden bursts of energy from the Sun that then travel through the solar system.

For the next few days, the astronauts were unable to leave the base. They had received warnings from Mission Control of a solar flare. These extra-strong rays of the Sun could kill them because the Martian atmosphere would not protect them as Earth's does.

Finally, CapCom gave them the all clear.

Lem, Izzy, and Alex set off eagerly on their quad bikes. This time, they headed for the North Pole. They had changed the bikes' wheels to the ones that could grip on sand dunes. It took them over half the day to cover the distance.

Mars is very cold. The **North Pole** is covered by dry ice and water ice. Dry ice is frozen carbon dioxide.

Alex set up the monitors right away to measure the depth of the dry ice.

"It's like stepping through clouds," remarked Izzy.

"It's hard to get any grip," said Lem, as he struggled to climb an arch-shaped sand dune. He slid back with each step he took.

"I'm not surprised. There's a layer of slippery sand and dust below this dry ice," replied Izzy.

Suddenly, the CapCom radio beeped.

"Hey guys! There's an asteroid coming your way. We estimate impact will be in less than twelve hours. You need to get off Mars and back to *Ramesses* NOW."

"Message received and understood," said Lem, urgently. "We'll head back to *Memphis* right away."

Asteroids [AS-ter-oids] are space rocks. There is a ring of millions of asteroids between Mars and the next outer planet, Jupiter.

The team sped back to base.

Without delay, they climbed into *Memphis*. Izzy placed Coconut safely inside her hutch in the hold.

Alex sat at the controls and fired up the booster rockets. *Memphis* rumbled as it lifted off the red planet.

On *Ramesses*, Flo and Ned were ready to meet them.

"Welcome back," they cried, as Alex, Lem, and Izzy appeared through the hatch.

"And just in time!" said Flo. "The asteroid hit Mars a few minutes ago and left a big crater."

"Mission Control has given us the go-ahead to continue the mission," said Ned, happily. "Next stop: Jupiter!"

Mars Data File

Location: fourth planet from the Sun

Landscape: rocky, barren, rust red, iron-rich ground

Size: just over half the size of Earth

Length of days: 24.6 Earth hours

Length of year: 687 Earth days

Dark slash around the equator is a long, deep canyon.

Dark circles are vast volcanoes; light ones are craters.

Frosty poles are covered in dry ice and water ice.